Steve Backlund's new book, *Declarations*, will wake you into new dimensions in God. It will shift the very foundation of what it means to come into agreement with the Kingdom of Heaven! If you want to transform the world with the power of your words and join the great adventure, then this book is for you!

Kris Vallotton
Senior Associate Leader, Bethel Church, Redding, CA
Co-Founder of Bethel School of Supernatural Ministry
Author of ten books, including The Supernatural Ways of Royalty and Spirit Wars

Declarations should be an important part of our spiritual grounding. As always, Steve's insight gives you the right tools to hit this topic well. This is an inspirational book that will teach you to walk in victory in every part of your life.

Beni Johnson
Author of The Happy Intercessor

One of the keys to the life of our church culture here at Bethel is we have a high value for making declarations. Steve in this new book, *Declarations,* does a great job of explaining and encouraging us to create more space in our life for declaring the things that matter to God and to us. Definitely would encourage you to read this book and to implement what you read. Enjoy!

Eric Johnson
Sr. Pastor, Bethel Church, Redding, CA

The youth of today need to learn how to direct their lives and discover their identity through this powerful and vital part of the Kingdom. I believe the declarations found in this book will be like a battering ram to the walls in your mind and dynamite to your faith!

Tom Crandall
Youth Pastor, Awakening, Bethel Church, Redding CA

Steve carries a contagious joy based on a theology that ends every sentence with "God is good." He electrified our church with a positive Kingdom outlook. This book is weaponry for successful battle through declaration, as well as preemptive strikes against wrong thinking and imaginations. Much of the 21st century church has divorced itself from the ancient Christian creeds and manifestos. This book is a collection of Biblically based creeds that will align your spirit with that which is in Heaven. I believe it will bring Heaven's stuff to earth's challenges. Read, speak, reap!

Steve Witt
Senior Leader, Bethel Cleveland, OH

It was a privilege given to me to receive this new book, *Declarations*, by Steve Backlund. It is another brick in the house of hope to add to Kingdom life. Steve has the great gift to articulate the truths of the Kingdom in a way that draw people into a life of hope. I have been so blessed to see those in our church who don't consider themselves to be readers, take these books and devour them. Steve writes in a way that gives God's people bite size pieces of revelation, which opens the doorway to a life of glistening hope. I absolutely believe that every saint should read this book. *The Thirty Biblical Reasons For Making Declarations* is stunning and worth the price of the book alone. I will keep this book by my bed and begin each day with a new key that will unlock for me the great future that my Father sees!

Pastor Andrew Magrath
Hope City Church, Australia

I absolutely loved *Declarations* by Steve Backlund. I think it's one of Steve's best books yet. I specifically loved the lists of declarations because they are so packed with truth. This book is going to set so many people free!

Jared Neusch
Third Year Overseer BSSM

Steve and Wendy visited our church in 2011, when we were somewhat "Joy Impaired." As a result of their trip and more recently by using the *Possessing Joy* book, we have been transformed and have started a journey into His fullness of Joy. We now use the book as a foundational module for everyone, what a Joy! We have found Steve's approach to unlocking truth in bite-sized chunks while releasing misconceptions very powerful and transforming. This latest book, *Declarations*, again surprises you with the simple yet powerful way it rearranges your thinking and unpacks truth, leaving your soul nourished and your thinking transformed. *Declarations* will change our lives and churches.

Kim & Liz McCaffery,
Leamington Spa, UK

Steve is fathering an audible revolution of agreement with God's word. *Declarations* accelerates the revolution, audibly demolishing the spirit of joylessness, poverty, marginal existence and isolation, propelling individuals, groups, businesses, governments and nations who would apply it into their God intended glory here on earth. You must join the revolution, it is changing the planet!

David Brudnicki
Urban Mission Church, Jersey City, NJ

In *Declarations*, Steve Backlund and his team open up the life-giving reality found in agreeing with God and speaking His mind over us, and our environment. Complete with both scriptural background and practical advice, I heartily recommend the truths presented in this book to any Christian who is seeking to follow God's call to change the spiritual weather system of an unreached culture.

Danny Turner
Church Planter, WEC Thailand

Declarations is a power-releasing book! My nation needs to understand the power of this message! I am very grateful for all the new knowledge I received through this book about declarations! I will most certainly be a more intentional thinker and speaker from now on!

Minna
Kouvola, Finland

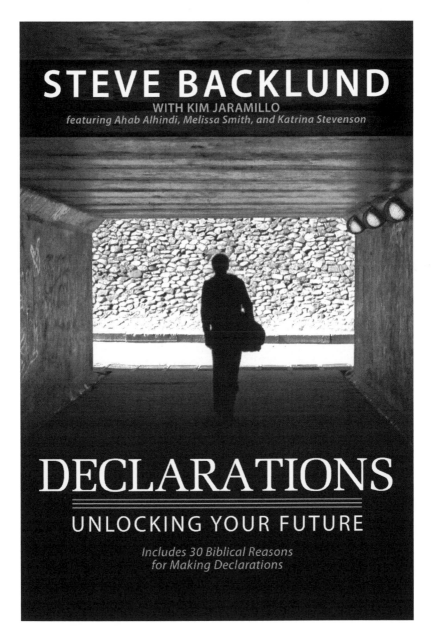

STEVE BACKLUND

WITH KIM JARAMILLO
featuring Ahab Alhindi, Melissa Smith, and Katrina Stevenson

DECLARATIONS
UNLOCKING YOUR FUTURE

*Includes 30 Biblical Reasons
for Making Declarations*

iGNITING
HOPE
MINISTRIES

Cover Design : Linda Lee www.LindaLeeCreates.com
Interior Design and Formatting : Lorraine Box PropheticArt@sbcglobal.net

Many thanks to the following people for their input in the writing of these devotionals:
Holly Hayes, Kim Jaramillo, Julie Mustard, and Elizabeth Preece.

ISBN: 978-0-9892066-1-7

DEDICATED

To every intern I have had from
September 2008 to May 2013

Thanks for making such a difference in my life and ministry.

2008-2009 — Josh Montovon

2009-2010 — Ron Day, Carl Richardson, Kaehler Sterr

2010-2011 — Phil Drysdale, Kim Jaramillo,
Chuck Maher, Jared Neusch

2011-2012 — Ahab Alhindi, Matt Coil, Jesse Cupp, Holly
Hayes, Anna Maher, Wendee Mannon, Melissa Smith, Chris
Smith, Katrina Stevenson, Elizabeth Villaseñor

2012-2013 — Heidi Anderson, Anne Ballard, Grace
Colledge, Jared Cullop, Levi Hug, Jaz Jacob, Julie Mustard,
Kevin Reagey, Elizabeth Reisinger, Jesse Skinner

CONTENTS

ABOUT THE AUTHORS

Steve Backlund

Steve Backlund was a senior pastor for seventeen years before joining the team at Bethel Church in Redding, California, in 2008. Steve is a revivalist teacher who calls people to higher perspectives through believing truth. At Bethel Church, he teaches leadership development in both the ministry school and through Global Legacy's Leadership Development online school. Steve and his wife, Wendy, are also the founders of Igniting Hope Ministries, which emphasizes joy, hope, and victorious mindsets through books, audio messages, and through their extensive travel.

Kim Jaramillo, *2011 intern*

After assisting Steve in the Church Leadership and Planting track in Bethel's School of Supernatural Ministry, Kim became Steve's Personal Assistant and the Program Manager of the Leadership Development Program for Global Legacy. She recently moved to Monterey with her husband, SPC Jaramillo, where she is impacting the lives of military wives and families.

Melissa Smith, *2012 intern*

After growing up in Michigan, Melissa spent several years on staff with Youth With A Mission before coming to Bethel. She and her husband, Chris, were both interns for Steve in their third year at Bethel's School of Supernatural Ministry and now work at Bethel Redding.

Ahab Alhindi, *2012 intern*

Ahab was born in New York and raised in Southern California. He and his wife Jessica are itinerate ministers for Bethel Church in Redding, California. In addition to their role in ministry, they own a local coffee shop and restaurant. Ahab's heart is to see the Kingdom of God flow in every part of society and to see the body of Christ walk in all her fullness.

Katrina Stevenson, *2012 intern*

Katrina is a revival group pastor at *Bethel School of Supernatural Ministry*. Prior to this, she interned for Steve as a Global Legacy Regional Catalyst, working to strengthen the apostolic relational network within the Pacific Northwest & Western Canada. Katrina is originally from Australia but spent nine years in London with her husband, Dave, prior to moving to Redding in 2009.

Kim, Steve, Katrina, Melissa, and Ahab

INTRODUCTION

"Why is the worship leader repeating that phrase over and over?"

As I thought about this, I believe God told me, "Because My people are not consistently declaring truth, I will cause songwriters to write songs with words they should be saying without music. This will give Me something powerful to work with in their lives and on planet earth."

So we sing repeatedly words like:

I am forgiven

Jesus is alive

He has set me free

I am alive in Him

I am the righteousness of Christ

I am healed by His stripes

As we sing these phrases, our mind is renewed, and we enter into a whole new realm of possibilities for our lives. This experience provides a revelation of how declarations (intentionally speaking truth) are a key for living a victorious and advancing life.

Declarations is a book divided into three parts.

- Thirty biblical reasons for making declarations

- Answering common objections to the making of declarations

- Thirty devotionals using declarations concerning ordinary areas of life

My fellow authors and I have designed *Declarations* to be easy to understand, overflowing with scripture, practical, and short in length. We have cut out the "fluff" in the book so the reader will receive the maximum experience in the shortest amount of time.

I no longer mind repeating those phrases over and over as I worship in song. I have taught on declarations for years now and have heard testimony after testimony of how adding this habit has been transformational to all kinds of people. We believe this book will change the lives of those who read it and put its teaching into practice.

Steve Backlund
Igniting Hope Ministries

HOW TO USE THIS BOOK

Thirty Biblical Reasons For Making Declarations

Saturate yourself with the verses listed. Meditate on the truths from these scripture passages. This is the most important part of the book because as you become convinced of the power of your words, you will be propelled to become an intentional speaker and develop your own system to make declarations.

Common Objections To The Making of Declarations

Many people question the teaching about declarations because of the poor lifestyle examples of some of its proponents and because of church teachings that oppose it. This section of the book is designed to answer some of the most common criticisms about the teachings of declarations (also called decrees and positive confession).

Devotionals For Different Areas Of Life

These are divided into five parts:

1. **The Title** – This is a familiar area of life that is important to target for the renewing of the mind and for transformation.

2. **The Scripture** – The declarations in the devotionals are based on truths in the Bible. Two or three of these are written here.

3. **The Declarations** – These are specific truths related to the topic of the devotional. Speak these out loud to help increase your faith in this area of life (Romans 10:17).

4. **The Breaking Off Of Agreement With These Common Lies** – Two lies are listed that frequently hinder people from believing God's truth in this aspect of life. Because God laughs at what His enemies say (Psalm 2:1-4), we suggest that you chuckle as well at these deceptions.

5. **The Wisdom To Add To The Declarations** – The making of declarations is only part of a good strategy for breakthrough and advancement. This section of the devotionals gives insight.

THIRTY BIBLICAL REASONS FOR MAKING DECLARATIONS

1. Life is in the power of the tongue.

"Death and life are in the power of the tongue, and those who love it will eat its fruit" (Proverbs 18:21). One of the greatest revelations we can ever get as we walk as believers is this: The tongue has power to release life wherever we go. Those who love this truth will speak intentionally and will eat the abundant fruit their past words (declarations) have produced. If we believe Proverbs 18:21, we will speak on purpose. We will speak to others and to ourselves because we realize there is no such thing as the strong silent type of Christian. Life and strength are accelerated through declarations.

2. Declarations "frame" our future.

"By faith we understand that the worlds were framed by the word of God, so that the things which are seen were not made of things which are visible" (Hebrews 11:3). Indeed our words influence the spirit realm (which ultimately impacts what we experience in the natural realm), but declarations are also a main building material to frame the "house" of our life destiny. Where do you want to be in five years? What do you want to build in you and through you? Declare now what it will look like. As you do, you are giving God a powerful framework to work with in you and in your life.

3. Words propel us to experience all that Jesus won for us.

"For by your words you will be justified, and by your words you will be condemned" (Matthew 12:37). This verse is obviously not talking about being saved through godly speaking, but it does imply that our declarations will either restrict or bless our lives. Words in agreement with God's purposes will propel us into the abundant life Jesus promised us. Instead of setting up fences of limitation and restriction in our experience (what Jesus calls being "condemned"), we will be able to enter into the realms of our salvation that we make declarations about.

4. Grace is imparted when we hear life-giving declarations.

"Let no corrupt word proceed out of your mouth, but what is good for necessary edification, that it may impart grace to the hearers" (Ephesians 4:29). Grace is the empowerment to do God's will. We have the privilege of continually imparting grace to others through our words, but because we are the one who hears our words the most, we can continually impart grace to ourselves through our words. Truly, there is no limit to how much grace we can receive from ourselves.

5. Declarations are a way to overcome anxiety and become glad.

"Anxiety in the heart of man causes depression, but a good word makes it glad" (Proverbs 12:25). It is a tremendous revelation when we understand we can speak a "good word" to ourselves to change our emotions from worry to gladness. Philippians 4:6-7 tells us that prayer with thanksgiving creates a life protected by peace. "Be anxious for nothing, but in everything by prayer and supplication, with thanksgiving, let your requests be made known to God; and the peace of God, which surpasses all understanding, will guard your hearts and minds through Christ Jesus." The phrase "with thanksgiving" could be interpreted as a type of declaration that declares with gratitude that God is working in the situations that concern us. So, whether we speak a good word to ourselves of "thank you" or speak a scriptural promise, we are privileged to have the weapon of declarations to make our hearts glad.

6. Abraham's history-changing example speaks of the power of declarations.

No longer shall your name be called Abram, but your name shall be Abraham; for I have made you a father of many nations" (Genesis 17:5). Abram means "exalted father," while Abraham means "Father of a multitude." God asked Abraham to call himself by His promises. He was to do this by declaring he was a father of a multitude even before he had one legitimate descendent. It is logical to conclude God actually changed Abraham's name to make sure that he would speak the promise, thus giving heaven something to work with. It is fascinating to note that the original promise was given at age 75, but nothing really happened until Abraham was 99 when he started declaring God's promise. This story speaks volumes to us about bringing long standing promises into our experience through declarations.

7. Faith comes by hearing truth, and declarations cause us to grow in our faith by regularly hearing truth.

"So then faith comes by hearing, and hearing by the word of God" (Romans 10:17). We don't have to wait for someone to speak in order to tap into this truth; in fact, we can determine the amount of hearing we would like to have through proactive speaking in our own lives. Jesus actually ties future abundance to the level of our hearing now. "Take heed what you hear. With the same measure you use, it will be measured to you" (Mark 4:24). One of the ways we can increase the level of our faith is by hearing our own frequent declarations.

8. Declarations direct our lives toward what we speak.

"Look also at ships: although they are so large and are driven by fierce winds, they are turned by a very small rudder wherever the pilot desires. Even so the tongue" (James 3:4-5). We are pulled in the direction of the words we speak. Our words are indeed a rudder to cause us to be directed toward the things we say. What destination do you want to be at in life in five years? Once you imagine it, begin by declaring it now, and the "ship" of your life will be directed toward that. I (Steve) had to say "I write books" before I ever wrote one. As I spoke this, the rudder of my life directed me toward book writing. As we consider this, it is important to know that the ship of your life includes you and your descendants. Many of your declarations will be fully fulfilled through your lineage (both physical and spiritual).

9. Declarations seal the realities of salvation into our lives.

"That if you confess with your mouth the Lord Jesus and believe in your heart that God has raised Him from the dead, you will be saved. For with the heart one believes unto righteousness, and with the mouth confession is made unto salvation" (Romans 10:9-10). Belief + confession = salvation. God's plan for getting us into the Kingdom and advancing in the Kingdom is the same: hear good news, believe it, and then declare (confess) its reality out of our mouths.

10. If we control our words, we can control our whole life.

James 3:2 is an incredible truth for the overcoming Christian. "For we all stumble in many things. If anyone does not stumble in word, he is a perfect man, able also to bridle the whole body" (James 3:2). We will change our lives when we change our words. Declarations are one way we can apply this astonishing truth. If we want to see an area of our lives positively transformed, then making specific declarations regarding that area is a way to start our plan to do so. Something powerful happens when we declare a scriptural reality for us.

11. Mountains move for those who believe they can have what they declare.

"For assuredly, I say to you, whoever says to this mountain, 'Be removed and be cast into the sea,' and does not doubt in his heart, but believes that those things he says will be done, he will have whatever he says" (Mark 11:23). The major truth of this verse is easy to miss. Jesus is not saying, "He who believes the mountain will be removed will see it done." No, He is releasing a much more powerful truth– "He who believes whatever he says will be done will have mountains move when he speaks." Read the verse again. Do you see it? This text alone will propel a lifestyle of declarations so that we can go on the journey to truly believe we have what we say.

12. We cannot just think our way out of the wilderness; we must speak our way out.

"Now when the tempter came to Him, he said, 'If You are the Son of God, command that these stones become bread.' But He answered and said, 'It is written, "Man shall not live by bread alone, but by every word that proceeds from the mouth of God"'" (Matthew 4:3-4). The way Jesus dealt with this temptation (and the two others listed in Matthew 4) illustrates the importance of speaking truth to defeat demonic lies. Those who only do battle against lies in their thoughts will find it much more challenging than those who include declarations in their truth journey. Intentional speaking of truth will bring forth some of the greatest victories.

13. Positive spiritual fires are started through declarations.

"The tongue is so set among our members that it defiles the whole body, and sets on fire the course of nature…" (James 3:6). Words are powerful. Death and life is in the power of the tongue (see Proverbs 18:21), but the greater truth is that life is in the power of the tongue. If negative words can cause the destruction described in James 3, then how much more can good words cause positive things? (Remember, God's positive is always greater than the devil's negative – see Romans 5:20). Those who make declarations will not only build up their own faith, but will also spark fires of revival and renewal wherever they speak.

14. Declarations keep us from reverting back to a performance based Christianity.

"O foolish Galatians! Who has bewitched you that you should not obey the truth, before whose eyes Jesus Christ was clearly portrayed among you as crucified? This only I want to learn from you: Did you receive the Spirit by the works of the law, or by the hearing of faith? Are you so foolish? Having begun in the Spirit, are you now being made perfect by the flesh? Have you suffered so many things in vain—if indeed it was in vain? Therefore He who supplies the Spirit to you and works miracles among you, does He do it by the works of the law, or by the hearing of faith?" (Galatians 3:1-5). These verses say the "hearing of faith" is the key to continuing in the Spirit and avoiding a "works of the law" focus. One of the best ways we can participate in this hearing of faith is to make declarations of the truth of our salvation – which comes by grace alone through faith.

15. Declarations unlock destinies.

"And the Angel of the Lord appeared to him, and said to him, 'The Lord is with you, you mighty man of valor!'" (Judges 6:12). Gideon's nation delivering leadership mantle was unlocked when the angel made a declaration over him of his true identity of who he really was. Gideon had a difficult time believing this at first, but eventually he did. We can become the angel in our own lives by declaring who we are in Christ, even when it seems and feels ridiculous (as it did to Gideon when he heard the angel). By calling ourselves what we are before we are, we unlock our future to greater possibilities.

16. Declarations establish what we desire to have in our lives.

"You will also declare a thing, and it will be established for you;

so light will shine on your ways" (Job 22:28). This passage says if we declare something, it will happen. Remember, we don't have something just by saying something, but saying something is necessary to having something. As part of our plan to establish a certain reality in our lives, we declare it as already happening (or that it will happen). We are given the promise that it will take place. We are also told, "Light will shine on our ways." When we declare, we will shine as lights in the world – illuminating the goodness and glory of God all around us.

17. Jesus began His supernatural ministry with declarations, so why wouldn't we?

"So He came to Nazareth, where He had been brought up. And as His custom was, He went into the synagogue on the Sabbath day, and stood up to read. And He was handed the book of the prophet Isaiah. And when He had opened the book, He found the place where it was written: 'The Spirit of the Lord is upon Me, because He has anointed Me to preach the gospel to the poor; He has sent Me to heal the brokenhearted, to proclaim liberty to the captives and recovery of sight to the blind, to set at liberty those who are oppressed; to proclaim the acceptable year of the Lord.' Then He closed the book, and gave it back to the attendant and sat down. And the eyes of all who were in the synagogue were fixed on Him. And He began to say to them, 'Today this Scripture is fulfilled in your hearing." (Luke 4:18-21). Jesus declared who He was before it was a reality in His experience. We are privileged to do the same.

18. Declarations are instrumental for us to enter our "Promised Land."

Joshua is our example to use declarations as a means to possessing the promises of God. "This Book of the Law shall not depart from your mouth, but you shall meditate in it day and night, that you may observe to do according to all that is written in it. For then you will make your way prosperous, and then you will have good success" (Joshua 1:8). Joshua was instructed to implement nonstop speaking (declaring) of truth as he made final preparations to possess what God had already given the Israelites through promise. This is true for you also. Joshua is our example to use declarations as a means to possessing the promises of God.

19. The centurion (whom Jesus celebrated) understood the power of a declaration.

"'Say the word, and my servant will be healed. For I also am a man placed under authority, having soldiers under me. And I say to one, "Go," and he goes; and to another, "Come," and he comes; and to my servant, "Do this," and he does it.' When Jesus heard these things, He marveled at him, and turned around saying and said to the crowd that followed Him, 'I say to you, I have not found such great faith, not even in Israel!' And those who were sent, returning to the house, found the servant well who had been sick" (Luke 7:7-10). Read this again: "Say the word and my servant will be healed." This is marvelous. The centurion understood something life-changing about the power of a faith-filled declaration. His revelation even surprised Jesus. Let's do the same.

20. Declarations are the opposite of speaking idle words.

"But I say to you that for every idle word men may speak, they will give account of it in the Day of Judgment" (Matthew 12:36). The writers of this book believe the main "giving of account" mentioned here is going to be the revelation of the power of the words we spoke in this life. We will be surprised at how a comment like, "I can't speak well in front of others," puts limitations around our potential in that area of life. These "idle words" that Jesus refers to are off-hand, unplanned comments that we make which hinder our lives and the lives of others. Declarations are the opposite of idle words because they are words in harmony with God's heart that are intentionally spoken. We will also see on the day we give account how saying something like "This is going to be a great day," actually helped our day become better than it would have been if we had not spoken it. Let's not wait until that day to be convinced of the power of our words; let's be convinced now.

21. He who would love life and see good days will make declarations.

"He who would love life and see good days, let him refrain his tongue from evil, and his lips from speaking deceit" (1 Peter 3:10). The first thing mentioned for those who want to see good in their lives is to control their speech. Wow, what a mighty promise this is! We remind you that controlling our words is not just stopping negative words, but more importantly, controlling our words is choosing to speak positively. Life truly is in the power of the tongue.

22. The weak are to declare they are strong.

"Let the weak say, 'I am strong'" (Joel 3:10). This passage tells the one who is having a weak experience to not agree with the experience, but to keep agreeing with God's truth. It is not about denying weakness. (It does not say, 'Let the weak say, "I am not weak."') We are to believe we are a strong person having a weak experience. We keep moving forward in our biblical identity by saying (declaring) we are strong, not only thinking it. The truth in Joel 3:10 is not an isolated truth about weakness, but it is a universal principle to be applied to every area of life. "Let the poor say, 'I am rich,'" or "Let the disorganized say, 'I am organized,'" or "Let the one who does not speak well in front of others say, 'I speak well in front of others.'" It is a key step in demolishing the lie that we are who our past experience says we are.

23. Declarations help us call those things that are not as though they are.

"(As it is written, 'I have made you a father of many nations') in the presence of Him whom he believed—God, who gives life to the dead and calls those things which do not exist as though they did" (Romans 4:17). God's method of bringing life to dead places, people, nations, gifts, and calls is for someone to say they are alive even when they still look dead. (The essence of faith is to believe before we see, not see to believe.) When we declare things alive that look dead, we become like God in "calling those things that are not as though they are."

24. Declarations help us to stay grounded in truth.

"Likewise you also, reckon yourselves to be dead indeed to sin, but alive to God in Christ Jesus our Lord" (Romans 6:11). Even though this verse does not state we are to declare as part of our reckoning, declaring certainly can be part of our plan to stay grounded in truths such as the finished work of the cross. Joshua kept focused on the truth through speaking as well. "This book of the law shall not depart from your mouth" (Joshua 1:8). As we talk to ourselves about biblical realities, our beliefs will become more deeply rooted in them.

25. We are called to be incessant hope speakers, and declarations help make this a reality in our lives.

"Let us hold fast the confession of our hope without wavering, for He who promised is faithful" (Hebrews 10:23). Note that it does not say, "Let us hold fast the 'thought' of our hope," but it says, "the confession of our hope." We are instructed to value and diligently protect the habit of speaking hope. There are many ways we can do this (encouraging others, sharing testimonies, being positive in conversations, etc.), but one of the most practical ways to follow this scripture is to regularly make declarations over ourselves, others, and every environment we find ourselves in.

26. Declarations are a way for us to pray believing prayers.

"Whatever things you ask when you pray, believe that you receive them, and you will have them" (Mark 11:24). An astounding spiritual principle is this: If we believe we have received the answer to our prayer at the time of asking, then we will see the answer. One of the best ways to demonstrate belief in past prayers is to make declarations that we have the things we have prayed for. I John 5:14-15 gives us insight in how this all works. "Now this is the confidence that we have in Him, that if we ask anything according to His will, He hears us. And if we know that He hears us, whatever we ask, we know that we have the petitions that we have asked of Him." With this verse in mind, here is a pattern for seeing God's promises fulfilled in your life: 1) Know God's will about specific areas of life through His promises in Scripture. 2) Ask for this to become reality in your life. 3) Declare it is reality before you see it.

27. Declarations give the Holy Spirit something to work with to accomplish God's will.

"The earth was without form, and void; and darkness was on the face of the deep. And the Spirit of God was hovering over the face of the waters. Then God said, 'Let there be light;' and there was light" (Genesis 1:2-3). Hear this truth: If something happened, then something was spoken. Both God and the devil need our words to accomplish their "wills" on earth. We have the privilege of speaking intentionally into chaotic areas of life and seeing chaos come into order. As we think of this reality, it would be fascinating to have our spiritual eyes opened to see the many areas the Spirit is hovering over that just need a word spoken for everything to change.

28. Giant killers make declarations.

"The Lord, who delivered me (David) from the paw of the lion and from the paw of the bear, He will deliver me from the hand of this Philistine… This day the Lord will deliver you into my hand, and I will strike you and take your head from you. And this day I will give the carcasses of the camp of the Philistines to the birds of the air and the wild beasts of the earth, that all the earth may know that there is a God in Israel. Then all this assembly shall know that the Lord does not save with sword and spear; for the battle is the Lord's, and He will give you into our hands" (1 Samuel 17:37, 46-47). David sets the example for us in using words to overcome fear and defeat seemingly impossible challenges to us. We can also employ this model as we "attack" every day with declarations like this, "Today the Lord will deliver to me an incredible day of breakthrough and miracles. I will have victory in everything I do." We are giant killers, so let's make declarations.

29. Declarations are a key to demolishing strongholds.

"For the weapons of our warfare are not carnal but mighty in God for pulling down strongholds, casting down arguments and every high thing that exalts itself against the knowledge of God, bringing every thought into captivity to the obedience of Christ" (2 Corinthians 10:4-5). The highest level of spiritual warfare is to take every thought captive to the obedience of Christ. One way to capture lies is to declare the truth that refutes the lies we are tempted to believe. We cannot think a lie when speaking truth. By making daily declarations, we pronounce truth and destroy negative strongholds and establish truth based belief systems.

30. The making of declarations is one of the most practical ways to renew our minds and build our faith.

"And do not be conformed to this world, but be transformed by the renewing of your mind" (Romans 12:2). The renewing of the mind does not happen by osmosis, but by an intentional plan to dismantle wrong beliefs and establish positive strongholds in specific areas of our lives. It is an irrefutable law of the Spirit that if we renew our minds, we will be transformed. It will work for everyone no matter what our past has been. (Truly, nobody's past can limit their future, but current beliefs can.) Besides meditating on Scripture, there is probably no greater strategic step we can take to renew our minds than making declarations. Declarations help us renew our minds to believe truth so our lives will be truly transformed. Remember, "Faith comes by hearing" (Romans 10:17), and we get to determine how much we hear by how much we declare.

BONUS SCRIPTURAL SUPPORT FOR THE MAKING OF DECLARATIONS

1. **The worlds were created with a declaration.**

   "The earth was without form, and void; and darkness was on the face of the deep. And the Spirit of God was hovering over the face of the waters. Then God said, 'Let there be light;' and there was light" (Genesis 1:2-3).

2. **The Spirit's anointing causes us to make declarations that set people free.**

   "The Spirit of the Lord God is upon Me, because the Lord has anointed Me to proclaim liberty to the captives, and the opening of the prison to those who are bound" (Isaiah 61:1).

3. **Declaring truth to others causes a chain reaction of breakthrough.**

   "Say to those who are fearful-hearted, 'Be strong, do not fear! Behold, your God will come with vengeance, With the recompense of God; He will come and save you.' Then the eyes of the blind shall be opened, and the ears of the deaf shall be unstopped. Then the lame shall leap like a deer, and the tongue of the dumb sing. For waters shall burst forth in the wilderness, and streams in the desert." (Isaiah 35:4-6).

4. Favor with God and man is established by making declarations.

"Let not mercy and truth forsake you; bind them around your neck, write them on the tablet of your heart, and so find favor and high esteem In the sight of God and man" (Proverbs 3:3-4). "My tongue is the pen of a ready writer" (Psalm 45:1).

COMMON OBJECTIONS TO THE MAKING OF DECLARATIONS

OBJECTION ONE — *Aren't declarations simply repackaged "Name it and claim it, blab it and grab it" heresy?*

Some object to the teaching about declarations because of abuses they have seen or things they have heard during the "positive confession" movement. The confession teaching gained prominence particularly in the 1980's through the influence of Word of Faith teachers like Kenneth Hagin, Kenneth Copeland, and Charles Capps. These men, and others like them, emphasized confessing God's promises as a key ingredient in the life of faith. This teaching was criticized (justly and unjustly) for reasons we will address, and some labeled it as "name it and claim it, blab it and grab it" hogwash.

Certainly, there were many poor examples by the proponents of positive confession teachings. One of the most common problems was the perception that confessions were mainly used for personal gain (money, Cadillacs, life of pleasure, etc.), instead of Kingdom advancement. Another negative characteristic of this movement was the tendency of people who embraced this teaching to be critical of others who made negative confessions. They often became self-appointed "word policemen" who stirred up fear or opposition to this teaching. Thirdly, these incessant promise speakers often overemphasized the power of words, while underemphasizing other important aspects of the Christian life. Finally, the message fell into disrepute because many of the confessions made by people did not happen, including some well-publicized situations where people actually died after refusing medical care because they were "standing on their confession."

While it is understandable why some would label it "name it and claim it, blab it and grab it" in an effort to discourage others from falling into what was perceived as error, it is unfortunate that most Christians seemed to "throw out the baby with the bath water" concerning the truth about declarations and positive confession. This inclination to overreact to perceived error is not unique to the positive confession movement, and, unfortunately, causes many to miss out on powerful truths that God is revealing to the church. Indeed, numerous fresh revelations are messy in their inception as the body of Christ seeks to walk in them. It is the wise believer who asks God what He is doing in controversial teachings before dismissing them because of apparent negative fruit. As we consider the teaching on positive confession, it is clear that God was revealing the power of words —

- *that life is truly in the power of the tongue* (Proverbs 18:21);
- *that confession is made unto salvation* (Romans 10:10);
- *that if we bridle our tongues, we can bridle our whole body (James 3:2);*
- *that faith comes by hearing* (Romans 10:17);
- *that God calls those things that do not exist as though they do* (Romans 4:17); and,
- *that speaking causes things to happen* (Genesis 1:3).

Yes, let's stay away from extremes in our declaration journey, but let's also be zealous in our implementing the speaking of God's promises over our lives.

OBJECTION TWO — *Isn't this just a formula that one can do apart from intimacy with God?*

Some object to the message about declarations because they believe it is a "formula." Their concern comes from an assessment that those who promote the making of declarations are saying we can have whatever we say, regardless of what else is happening in our lives. It is seen as a formula to receive spiritual blessings without a covenant commitment to the Lord.

This same criticism could also be directed at many other Christian disciplines (i.e. Bible reading, tithing, prayer, church attendance, fellowship, loving your spouse, honesty, hard work, etc.). These, too, can become formulas for Christian success even if the individual does not have a current vibrant relationship with Jesus.

Godly principles work at some level for the saved and unsaved alike. Those who practice godly disciplines dramatically increase the likelihood of living a blessed life. Declarations (speaking life) certainly fall into the category of godly disciplines.

The "that's just a formula" label gets placed on positive proclaimers (more so than other disciplines) because the anti-negative speech advocates tend to be more vocal about their convictions, and their imbalances seem to be more obvious. They've boiled life down to this: Say the right words and everything will turn out wonderfully.

Yes, the belief that our words are powerful is one of the most important truths we will ever believe, but the authors of this book want it to be clear that declarations are one piece of the pie of truth, not the whole pie. The truths shared in these writings are to be lived out in tension with other important teachings. They are also to be lived out in the context of a community where healthy relationships are fostered. This will help prevent us from simply using declarations as a formula.

OBJECTION THREE — *Can't declarations be a presumptuous attempt to override God's sovereignty in our lives?*

This question goes to the heart of whether or not we believe our beliefs and actions actually influence what happens on planet earth and impacts the quality of our lives. There are two extremes concerning this. On one side, there are those who believe our lives are completely predestined by God and cannot be altered. On the other hand, some feverishly proclaim we can have whatever we speak without any acknowledgment of the larger purpose God might have for us. The authors of this book believe the answer is somewhere in between these perspectives and would emphasize much more a person's ability to create history rather than be a robotic pawn. Yes, "A man's steps are of the Lord" (Proverbs 20:24), but it is clear throughout scripture that we have been given delegated authority by God to:

- *increase our talents* (see Matthew 25:14-30),
- *control the devil's activity* (see James 4:7),
- *hasten the return of Christ* (see 2 Peter 3:12),
- *increase personal prosperity* (see Psalm 1:1-3),
- *bring peace and blessing to our cities* (see 1 Timothy 2:1-4), and
- *remove spiritual mountains with our words and faith* (see Mark 11:22-24).

Each of us will need to work out for ourselves how we balance the truth of God's sovereignty with the great God-given spiritual weapon of declarations to make things happen for ourselves and others. It is important to understand that we won't have something just because we say something, but saying something is vital for having something.

OBJECTION FOUR — *Aren't those who make declarations and positive confessions prone to being unrealistic and are often in denial about circumstances that need obedience and action, not just a declaration?*

Certainly these concerns are valid if someone is standing on their confession while ignoring other scriptural principles (or a serious medical diagnosis) about the situation. Even though we don't want to walk in foolishness in our declaration journey, it is important to also realize that God has not called us to be realistic but to live life as He sees it. We do not deny the negative facts of a situation, but we are to declare God's truth that is higher than the facts. Joel 3:10 is an example of this, "Let the weak say I am strong." It does not say, "Let the weak say I am not weak." We don't deny weakness, but we declare the truth of strength before it has manifested into reality. Declarations thus become an important part of our plan to build our faith to experience all that Jesus has made possible for us to walk in.

OBJECTION FIVE — *I tried it, and it felt fake to me.*

Some have attempted to make declarations in the past, and it just did not feel right; therefore, they quit. As we consider this, there are two things to remember: First, it is important to realize that many beneficial habits are not exciting in the beginning (for example exercise, nutrition, etc.). It often takes time to get over the initial discomfort. Secondly, because declarations are so powerful in demolishing negative strongholds in our minds, we should not be surprised at the resistance these long enduring belief systems put up. They just don't want to go. Even so, as you persevere in declaring truth, the confirming feelings will come.

OBJECTION SIX — *I tried it, and it did not work.*

Throughout the Word, God promises a good result if we heed certain truths He presents to us. For instance, "Give and it will be given to you" (Luke 6:38) or "'Honor your father and mother that it may go well with you and you may live long on the earth" (Ephesians 6:2-3). We are challenged to choose a certain course of action and then expect a positive outcome as a result. There are numerous verses in the Bible such as Proverbs 18:21 that tell us to anticipate blessing as we speak words of life. "Death and life are in the power of the tongue; and those who love it will eat its fruit." As with any spiritual discipline, we must persevere and overcome the perception that nothing is happening when we make declarations. "Whatever a man sows, that he will also reap . . . and let us not grow weary while doing good, for in due season we shall reap if we do not lose heart" (Galatians 6:7-9). The losing of heart comes from a belief that nothing is improving. We believe it is impossible to be relentless in declaring truth and not have forward movement in life and in the things of God.

30

DECLARATIONS

UNLOCKING YOUR FUTURE

1 JOY AND LAUGHTER

THE SCRIPTURE

"The joy of the Lord is your strength" (Nehemiah 8:10).

"A merry heart does good, like medicine" (Proverbs 17:22).

"In Your presence is fullness of joy" (Psalm 16:11).

THE DECLARATIONS

- I am an outrageously joyful person.

- My joy level is increasing daily, and I have been created to experience fullness of joy.

- Even in the midst of uncertainty, I live from a place of unshakeable joy.

- My joy levels do not depend on circumstances or how I feel.

- I love to laugh out loud, and I purpose to do so frequently.

- I experience great joy in my life even before I see the breakthroughs I am believing for.

- I naturally know when to "weep with those who weep" and "rejoice with those who rejoice."

- I am a carrier of infectious joy, and I release joy to others.

- My joy & laughter are powerful weapons of spiritual warfare and help create breakthrough in my own life and the lives of those around me.

- I reject foreboding and embrace hope and joy.

- I am building a stronghold of joy in my life.

THE BREAKING OFF OF AGREEMENT WITH THESE COMMON LIES

- I am not an outwardly joyful person.

- The Lord is not overly concerned with us experiencing joy.

THE WISDOM TO ADD TO DECLARATIONS

Choose joy — Just as we choose to forgive or to love, we can choose to be joyful. It is a spiritual muscle we can develop in our lives.

Act more joyful and enthusiastic than you feel — Your emotions will soon catch up to your actions. Know that you are not being "fake" in doing this – it is your true nature to be joyful!

In difficult situations, take time to laugh — When pressure is mounting, take 30 to 60 seconds to laugh out loud. This releases endorphins, reduces stress, and helps bring a clearer perspective. Make the ability to laugh in difficult situations a core value in your life.

BIBLICAL REASON #1

Proverbs 18:21
Life is in the power of the tongue.

2   TOMORROW

THE SCRIPTURE

"But as for me and my house, we will serve the Lord" (Joshua 24:15).

"Eye has not seen, nor ear heard, nor have entered into the heart of man the things which God has prepared for those who love Him"
(I Corinthians 2:9).

"One thing I do, forgetting those things which are behind and reaching forward to those things which are ahead" (Philippians 3:13).

THE DECLARATIONS

- Tomorrow is going to be one of the best days of my life.

- I will wake up with strong faith, strong love, and strong hope in my heart.

- I will exercise, eat right, drink much water, and laugh frequently tomorrow.

- God's Kingdom will advance everywhere I go and in everything I do.

- I will be extremely effective in my work tomorrow.

- I will have life-changing, secret place times with the Lord tomorrow.

- My past prayers will be working mightily tomorrow in every situation that concerns me.

- Right now, I demolish double-mindedness and a lack of enthusiasm I have about any activity, appointment, or meeting I have tomorrow.

- I will reach forward tomorrow to the things that are ahead of me.

- I will be victorious in everything I face tomorrow.

- I will make great decisions tomorrow in every situation I face.

THE BREAKING OFF OF AGREEMENT WITH THESE COMMON LIES

- I will need to wait until tomorrow to determine how I feel in order for me to know if it is going to be a good day.

- Making declarations today will not affect the quality of my tomorrow.

THE WISDOM TO ADD TO DECLARATIONS

Build faith through very specific declarations — We can release great faith for everything we do tomorrow by declaring over each activity we plan to do. As we make declarations, faith will rise in our hearts toward what you will do. This faith will cause greater impact to occur.

Take time to plan — Five minutes of planning for tomorrow will dramatically increase the likelihood of success for the day. As we plan, we can make sure that we have included in our schedule the activities that really matter and prepare accordingly.

Learn from today — During your planning and declaring for tomorrow, ask God this question: "What did I learn from today that will help me have a better tomorrow?" He loves answering that question!

BIBLICAL REASON #2

Hebrews 11:3
Declarations frame our future.

3 FAVOR OF GOD

THE SCRIPTURE

"For You, O Lord, will bless the righteous; With favor You will surround him as with a shield" (Psalms 5:12).

"And Jesus increased in wisdom and stature, and in favor with God and men" (Luke 2:52).

THE DECLARATIONS

- The favor of God is a shield in my life, keeping me from harm.

- I have an anointing that causes others to walk in abundant favor.

- Today is the day that God is going to show off His favor on me.

- My family and I are magnets of God's favor.

- The favor in my family increases with each new generation.

- Because I steward today's favor well, I am entrusted with more tomorrow.

- I am constantly stumbling into the favor of God.

- I have unusual favor in business, family, evangelism, with my neighbors, with political leaders, and in all areas of my life.

- People are drawn to me and instinctively like me.

- I am not limited to my current level of favor; my favor can and will grow.

- I effortlessly receive the favor of God through His grace.

THE BREAKING OFF OF AGREEMENT WITH THESE COMMON LIES

- I have been predetermined by God to not have significant favor.

- My favor is more dependent upon my performance than my beliefs.

THE WISDOM TO ADD TO DECLARATIONS

Steward your current level of favor well — Examine your life and find out where you see the favor of God. Once you discover where you are experiencing His favor, give thanks, and look for opportunities to use that favor to bless and benefit others.

Honor and celebrate the favor on others — Where you see God's favor being released through the people around you, encourage them in this, knowing that celebrating the blessings of others brings increase in your own life.

Be faithful in the small things of life — If you do small things in a great way (*for example* manage your time well, do what you say you will do, under-promise and over-deliver, etc.), you will grow in favor with God and man.

BIBLICAL REASON # 3

Matthew 12:37
Words justify us to experience all that Jesus won for us.

4   LOVING OTHERS

THE SCRIPTURE

"If we love one another, God abides in us, and His love has been perfected in us" (I John 5:12).

"Love never fails" (1 Corinthians 13:8).

THE DECLARATIONS

- I am known in heaven and on earth as one who loves well.

- My life overflows with God's love, making it impossible for me not to love others.

- Instead of allowing issues in the lives of others to be a barrier, I choose to love people into wholeness.

- People's responses to me do not determine how I love them.

- I have a gift for seeing through the dirt and finding the gold in others.

- One of my greatest joys in life is showing extravagant love to my family, friends, neighbors, work colleagues, acquaintances, and random strangers.

- I have great wisdom in knowing when to set boundaries that establish what I can and cannot do in loving others.

- My ability to love is not dependent upon how I feel or circumstances in my life.

- I am permanently tapped into Heaven's infinite supply of love.

THE BREAKING OFF OF AGREEMENT WITH THESE COMMON LIES

- If I show love toward someone before they clean up the mess in their life, they will have no incentive to improve.

- My prophetic gift allows me to easily see what's wrong with people therefore making it difficult for me to love them.

THE WISDOM TO ADD TO DECLARATIONS

Become continuously aware of God's love for you — It's His love for you that empowers you to love others (see 1 John 4:19). The more we experience His love, the easier we love others.

Learn to love yourself — The Scripture "You shall love your neighbor as yourself" (Mark 12:31) reveals loving ourselves as being a vital key that helps us love others.

Believe in the power of love — Even the most difficult person to love is longing to be loved. The very act of you loving them will help them put down their defenses and step into their God-given identity.

BIBLICAL SUPPORT #4

Ephesians 4:29
Grace is imparted when we hear life-giving declarations.

5

PEACE

THE SCRIPTURE

"Peace I leave with you; My peace I give to you..." (John 14:27).

"You will keep in perfect peace all who trust in you" (Isaiah 26:3).

THE DECLARATIONS

- I speak to any worry, stress, or anxiety, and I say you cannot stay. Peace reigns in this temple.

- Because I trust in God, I am kept in perfect peace.

- I am known as a peace carrier at home, in the work place, and in all areas of my life.

- I have a unique ability to remain peaceful, even as responsibilities increase.

- I do not have to strive for peace, as God has already given it to me.

- I bring peace to extremely intense situations.

- Those who experience anxiety claim it leaves when they come in contact with me.

- My home is filled with a tangible peace. When I walk in, I immediately feel at ease and calm.

- My heart and mind are guarded and protected by God's peace.

- My family is blessed with peace.

THE BREAKING OFF OF AGREEMENT WITH THESE COMMON LIES

- It is impossible to carry peace while having numerous responsibilities or when I am in stressful situations.

- My life has to be in order before I can experience peace.

THE WISDOM TO ADD TO DECLARATIONS

Meditate on Scripture — Look up peace in a concordance. Take time to think on the meanings of scriptures like Philippians 4:6-7, Matthew 11:28-30, John 14:27, and 2 Thessalonians 3:16.

Position yourself — Take five minutes in the morning to ask the Lord to fill you with His peace. Schedule two minute "peace breaks" throughout your day. Pause during those times and thank God for His peace.

Learn practical ways to grow in peace — Here are some good places to start: fellowship, exercise, budget your finances, plan your time, open a savings account, get out of debt, and prioritize time for healthy relationships.

BIBLICAL REASON #5

Proverbs 12:25
Declarations are a way to overcome anxiety and become glad.

6 PERSEVERANCE

THE SCRIPTURE

"And not only that, but we also glory in tribulations, knowing that tribulation produces perseverance; and perseverance, character; and character, hope. Now hope does not disappoint, because the love of God has been poured out in our hearts by the Holy Spirit who was given to us" (Romans 5:3-5).

THE DECLARATIONS

- There is always a solution.

- I am well able to overcome all challenges.

- Regardless of the storms that may surround me, I always have peace inside.

- I think long term, I visualize the end, and I see victory.

- I live with an expectation for the goodness of God to manifest, even in the most difficult times.

- Even when I feel like quitting, I push on towards the goal.

- I have an incredible ability to inspire others to walk in perseverance.

- I live a life of excellence.

- I not only start well in what I do, but I also finish well.

- Even when it seems that others do not believe in me, I know God believes in me.

THE BREAKING OFF OF AGREEMENT WITH THESE COMMON LIES

- Because my feelings are always right, if I don't feel like doing something, then I should stop doing it.

- Perseverance is code for God punishing me.

THE WISDOM TO ADD TO DECLARATIONS

Develop the habit of follow through — Find a way to consistently do the things you say you will do. (This is one of the most important steps to becoming a great influencer.) When you cannot fulfill a commitment, communicate as soon as possible with those affected.

Get a burning vision for your life — Athletes persevere through rigorous training because of a dream to win a championship. As we believe we are being prepared for something significant, we will be motivated to overcome obstacles in our way.

Understand our current assignment in life — We can overcome many negative circumstances if we know we are doing what God wants us to do. Noah persevered in building the ark because he heard from God. The Apostle Paul tenaciously overcame great problems because he knew the assignment God had given him. Strength comes when we conquer double-mindedness and recommit to what God has said.

BIBLICAL SUPPORT #6

Genesis 17:5
Abraham's history-changing example speaks of the power of declarations.

7 HEARING GOD'S VOICE

THE SCRIPTURE

"Your ears shall hear a word behind you, saying, 'This is the way, walk in it,'" (Isaiah 30:21).

"…'Man shall not live by bread alone, but by every word that proceeds from the mouth of God'" (Matthew 4:4).

THE DECLARATIONS

- My Father desires to speak to me even more than I desire to hear from Him.

- As a child of God, it is my privilege and birthright to hear my Father's voice.

- It is easy for me to hear the voice of God.

- Whatever God says to do is the most loving, most fruitful, and most exciting thing I can do.

- I am constantly hearing God's voice through scripture, my thoughts, other people, and nature.

- Even when my mind cannot comprehend, God is speaking to my spirit.

- When God speaks direction to me, He also provides the grace to do what He has said.

- As I renew my mind, God will reveal His good, pleasing, and perfect will to me.

- Hearing God's voice and obeying in faith is worth any risk of failure.

- As I attach faith to what I am hearing, He will do exceeding more than I could ever hope or imagine.

THE BREAKING OFF OF AGREEMENT WITH THESE COMMON LIES

- God doesn't speak to me as profoundly as He does to others.

- If I mishear the Lord on a major decision, I will automatically ruin my life.

THE WISDOM TO ADD TO DECLARATIONS

Thank Him for the ways He speaks to you now — This could be through Scripture, a sense of peace, or an encouraging word. Ask Him to open your spiritual "ears" to hear more from Him.

Start listening — Start listening for His voice on smaller issues to grow your faith in His ability to speak and your ability to hear.

Involve wise counsel — Share what you believe you are hearing with seasoned believers and see if they agree it lines up with Scripture, His character, and seems good to their spirit (Acts 15:28).

BIBLICAL SUPPORT #7

Romans 10:17
Faith comes by hearing truth, and declarations cause us to grow in our faith by regularly hearing truth.

8 DECISION MAKING

THE SCRIPTURE

"If any of you lacks wisdom, let him ask of God, who gives to all liberally and without reproach, and it will be given to him" (James 1:5).

THE DECLARATIONS

- I am a great decision-maker.

- The decisions I make today are producing blessing for my future generations.

- I make decisions about the future in confidence and trust in the goodness of my Father.

- I give no place to double-mindedness or regret as I make decisions.

- Every decision I make blesses the people around me and expands God's Kingdom on the earth.

- God wants me to make great decisions even more than I want to make them.

- I have an excellent process in decision-making that includes Scripture and the wisdom of key people in my life.

- I have a great anointing to lead others into the process of good decision-making.

- I am protected from impulsive choices.

- Any bad decision of the past is now being supernaturally worked out for my good and for God's glory.

- Like Jesus, when I am making a decision, I look to see what the Father is doing and saying.

THE BREAKING OFF OF AGREEMENT WITH THESE COMMON LIES

- Poor decisions I've made in the past are hindering God's plans from being accomplished in my life.

- There is only one path I can take to be in God's will for my life, and it is very narrow and difficult to discern.

THE WISDOM TO ADD TO DECLARATIONS

Develop a good process in decision making — A good method could flow in this order: Ground yourself in Scripture, include godly people in the process, list reasons for your decisions, make decisions in your heart and give God time to redirect. Give time for God to speak to you.

Begin making small decisions and choices with great faith — The next time you make a decision, believe God is going to bless your decision and work the results out for your good. See how this increases your faith for making bigger decisions.

Receive God's wisdom and strength to defeat these enemies of good decision-making — 1) Impulsiveness. 2) Fear of making a wrong decision. 3) Double-mindedness after decision-making. 4) Spending too much time with and being influenced negatively by those making bad choices in life. 5) Not including key people in your decision-making process (those affected by the decision, those who can help you, etc.).

BIBLICAL SUPPORT #8

James 3:4-5
Declarations direct our lives toward what we speak.

9 EVANGELISM

THE SCRIPTURE

"The Lord is... longsuffering toward us, not willing that any should perish but that all should come to repentance" (2 Peter 3:9).

"But you shall receive power when the Holy Spirit has come upon you; and you shall be witnesses to Me in Jerusalem, and in all Judea and Samaria, and to the end of the earth" (Acts 1:8).

THE DECLARATIONS

- Everywhere I go I am overwhelmed by the love of God for people and am highly motivated to share the gospel.

- It is easy and normal for me to articulate the gospel.

- I have an anointing for evangelism.

- Today my mind and spirit will tune into the people around me and find those who desire to be saved. I will lead those people to Jesus.

- I am fearless, courageous, and I live with an understanding that people are hungry for Jesus.

- I am creative in my evangelism, and I adapt well to bring powerful God-encounters to different kinds of people.

- I LOVE evangelizing.

- My family respects me and wants to hear from me because my Christian life is so attractive to them. It is easy to share the gospel with them because they want to know the God that is inside of me.

- My reputation for leading people to Jesus is so widely known in my town that when people want to get saved, they find me.

- When I feel afraid to share the gospel with someone, I will remind myself that on the other side of fear is a testimony.

THE BREAKING OFF OF AGREEMENT WITH THESE COMMON LIES

- People are fine the way they are, and they do not really want to get saved.

- I do not have a gifting to lead people to the Lord.

THE WISDOM TO ADD TO DECLARATIONS

Take steps to grow in confidence in sharing the gospel — 1) Daily practice. Say a simple gospel message in 30 seconds in front of the mirror. *2)* Take a class. There are schools and classes on evangelism that make it practical and easy. 3) Read a book. Learn how others have overcome obstacles to reach people for Christ.

Spend time with those who are effective evangelists — The best evangelism training is caught, not taught. True evangelists can instill traits in you like loving and enjoying people, "reading" people well, and knowing how far to go in conversations. Try starting conversations with people you do not know and see what happens.

Take small risks everyday — Do this until it begins to feel comfortable, then move into larger risks. Then just ask, "Would you like to give your life to Jesus?" You will be shocked at the results.

BIBLICAL REASON #9

Romans 10:9-10
Declarations seal the realities of salvation into our lives.

10 PERSONAL GROWTH

THE SCRIPTURE

"I have been crucified with Christ; it is no longer I who live, but Christ lives in me; and the life which I now live in the flesh I live by faith in the Son of God." (Galatians 2:20).

"So God created man in His own image; in the image of God He created him." (Genesis 1:27).

THE DECLARATIONS

- Intentionality is key to my personal growth. Everyday I do something that develops me.

- I am growing daily in my character, integrity, love, organization, communication, and leadership.

- I regularly read books and listen to talks on personal development that cause me to grow exponentially.

- I set measurable attainable goals for my growth.

- The Lord is causing me to grow without me even knowing the extent of it.

- I am committed to a life-long personal growth plan.

- I am a catalyst for personal growth in others.

- I have a community of people I invest in and grow with.

- I regularly review my growth, and I celebrate progress, not perfection.

- I restart my growth plan quickly when I have struggled.

- As I focus on Jesus and spend time in His presence, I am being transformed into His likeness.

THE BREAKING OFF OF AGREEMENT WITH THESE COMMON LIES

- There are too many areas in my life needing change, so it is not even worth trying.

- I've focused on personal growth in the past, but it didn't help. I am who I am, and I'll never change.

THE WISDOM TO ADD TO DECLARATIONS

Allow Holy Spirit to bring up key areas of growth to focus on — It is easy to get discouraged if we approach personal growth on our own and in our strength. God will always provide the grace we need to develop in areas He is highlighting.

Partner with others in your personal growth journey — It is simpler to grow and change if we do it with others who are passionate about personal growth. These "growth catalysts" can encourage us and help us see things from another perspective. They can also motivate us when we grow weary.

Consume books and audio messages that will inspire your growth — Take advantage of key moments in life to feed on inspiring messages (*for example* when getting ready in the morning, waiting for an appointment, driving in your car, while exercising, etc.).

BIBLICAL REASON #10

James 3:2
If we control our words, we can control our whole life.

11 GENEROSITY

THE SCRIPTURE

"That you, always having all sufficiency in all things, may have an abundance for every good work." (2 Corinthians 9:8)

"Give, and it will be given to you. A good measure, pressed down, shaken together and running over, will be poured into your lap." (Luke 6:38)

THE DECLARATIONS

- I am blessed, and I rejoice in blessing others.

- I am generous with my time, even during the busy seasons of life.

- I overflow with delight as I generously give to the Lord and to others.

- I am on a generosity rampage, seeking whom I can bless next.

- I do not worry about lack, knowing God will supply richly all of my needs; therefore, I am able to sow freely and liberally.

- Because I give, I expect a return that is of good measure, pressed down, shaken together, running over, and pouring out.

- I give grace generously to myself, and to those in my family. I am generous with my love, patience, and kindness.

- Because I carry the DNA of my heavenly Father, and because He is a generous Daddy, my DNA is infused with generosity.

- I have a unique ability to know when God is highlighting someone I should bless generously with time, money, or another resource.

- When others are generous towards me, I receive it with gladness.

THE BREAKING OFF OF AGREEMENT WITH THESE COMMON LIES

- If I am generous towards others with my time, money, or any other resource, I will run out of those things for myself or for my family.

- It is difficult for me to receive generosity from God or others.

THE WISDOM TO ADD TO DECLARATIONS

Generosity is not just about money — It's a willingness to give liberally. Ask Jesus who you should show generosity to and how to be generous. For example, give liberally of your time with someone you know in a nursing home, or give of your skill by donating three free piano lessons to someone eager to learn.

Receive generosity well — When others bless you, thankfully receive it, knowing that you are blessed to be a blessing, and that the person being generous with you will be blessed by sowing into you.

Know there are times not to give — Some get into trouble through continual impulsive giving that causes them to have nothing left for the well-being of themselves or for those who depend on them. If you find yourself regularly suffering financially because you give too much, create a monthly budget and designate an amount you can use monthly to give. Keep that amount in an envelope, and only give from that money when you feel led to be generous.

BIBLICAL REASON #11

Mark 11:23
Mountains move for those who believe they can have what they declare.

12 NO DIFFERENCE BETWEEN SACRED AND SECULAR

THE SCRIPTURE

"Whatever you do, work heartily, as for the Lord and not for men, knowing that from the Lord you will receive the inheritance as your reward. You are serving the Lord Christ" (Colossians 3:23-24).

"But we urge you, brethren that you increase more and more; that you aspire to lead a quiet life, to mind your own business, and to work with your own hands, as we commanded you, that you may walk properly toward those who are outside, and that you may lack nothing" (I Thessalonians 4:10-12).

THE DECLARATIONS

- Every single area of my life is sacred to the Lord.

- God does not see my secular job as less spiritual than vocational ministry.

- I honor God by loving people, living healthy, and by doing everything to the best of my abilities.

- God is fully interested and cares about all areas of my life. There is no area that He cares about less than another.

- Every single thing I do can be pleasing and acceptable worship to the Father.

- Because I do everything in faith, all I do is significant.

- Every person has a unique and significant purpose in life.

- God is calling powerful people to be in the arts, education, business, and other arenas of life.

- Ministry is not just something we do through the church, but it occurs in business, education, family, and many other areas of life.

- God's love for me is not dependent upon the job that I have.

THE BREAKING OFF OF AGREEMENT WITH THESE COMMON LIES

- Jobs in realms like business or education are not spiritual callings.

- If only I was in full-time vocational ministry, I could have more favor.

THE WISDOM TO ADD TO DECLARATIONS

Ask God for His perspective on what you do — Take some time to hear God's thoughts about your profession and/or passions. Let Him show you how valuable and spiritual it is. Write down what He says.

Partner with others — Find believers who are called into the same vocation as you are, and begin partnering with them by praying for one another, making declarations over each other, and sharing testimonies.

Become the best at what you do — No matter what you are called to, God has a plan to see you be successful and influence those in your field at high levels. Study, take classes, and seek mentoring to become excellent in this vocation. As you do everything unto the Lord, you will see your influence grow. See the people at your vocation as your mission field to love, serve, and release the supernatural everywhere you go.

BIBLICAL REASON #12

Matthew 4:3-4
We cannot just think our way out of the wilderness, but we must speak our way out.

13 INFLUENCING OTHERS IN A POSITIVE WAY

THE SCRIPTURE

"He who believes in Me, the works that I do he will do also; and greater works than these he will do" (John 14:12).

"You shall be witnesses to Me in Jerusalem, and in all Judea and Samaria, and to the end of the earth" (Acts 1:8).

THE DECLARATIONS

- Jesus influenced the world dramatically, and so do I.

- Just as Peter's shadow caused healing in Acts 5, my very presence releases miraculous transformation to those around me.

- There is no limit to the types of people and situations I impact.

- My life causes multitudes to surrender their lives to Jesus.

- My influence will be felt for hundreds of years.

- Because God's covenants are not limited by my lifespan, my whole family tree is altered. My descendants will be great leaders and influencers.

- Just as Obed Edom was blessed by the Ark of the Covenant dwelling in his house (see 2 Samuel 6:11), my city is blessed by me living in it.

- I value and understand the needs of people; therefore, I have great favor and influence.

- My hope, my finances, my strategies, and my partnerships with others are causing great positive change in lives and nations.

- It is impossible for people to be around me and not be changed.

THE BREAKING OFF OF AGREEMENT WITH THESE COMMON LIES

- I am a victim of other people's perceptions of me. If people saw me differently, then I could have influence.

- My past level of influence determines my future potential.

THE WISDOM TO ADD TO DECLARATIONS

Be baptized in the power of God — The book of Acts demonstrates how ordinary people can turn the world upside down if they have a life changing encounter with God's power. (See Acts 2, 8, and 19.)

Know that trust is the currency of long-lasting influence — We become more influential when we are perceived to be authentic, consistent, loving, and a positive change agent.

Increase your hope and your resources — Our hope level will ultimately determine our influence level. Also, as we increase in Kingdom abundance, we will be able to affect more lives.

BIBLICAL REASON # 13

James 3:6 and Proverbs 18:21
Positive spiritual fires are started through declarations.

14 BIBLE READING

THE SCRIPTURE

"Your Word is a lamp to my feet and a light to my path" (Psalm 119:105).

"As for God, His way is perfect; the word of the Lord is proven. He is a shield to all who trust in Him" (Psalm 18:30).

THE DECLARATIONS

- I love reading Scripture as a part of my daily routine.

- Every time I open the Bible, I receive fresh revelation and insight.

- There is nothing I am facing that Scripture cannot speak into.

- I have strong motivation and spiritual hunger to spend time in the Bible.

- Even Scriptures I have read hundreds of times come alive as I read them again.

- Every aspect of my life is impacted through the time I spend meditating on Scripture.

- It is easy for me to communicate what I am learning from the Bible.

- I claim and receive the promises of Scripture for my life and for my descendants.

- It's impossible for me to spend time in God's Word and not be radically transformed.

- I encounter God's love and power every time I am in His Word.

THE BREAKING OFF OF AGREEMENT WITH THESE COMMON LIES

- My life is too busy for me to fit in consistent time in the Word.
- The Bible is boring and irrelevant.

THE WISDOM TO ADD TO DECLARATIONS

Get a plan that works for you — 1) Find a translation you understand. 2) Become consistent with a small amount of daily reading, rather than trying to read huge amounts some days and none the next. 3) If you are unfamiliar with the Bible, start with the Gospel of John. Then proceed to Acts and the rest of the New Testament (mixing in Psalms and Proverbs as you are able).

Partner with others in your Bible-reading journey — Find a friend or small group to share your insights from Scripture with. It is much easier to dive into the Bible with others.

Apply these basics in interpreting the Bible — 1) Understand the finished work of the cross as described in Romans, Galatians, Ephesians and Colossians. 2) Take this understanding and let it help you interpret the Old Testament and the gospels (Matthew, Mark, Luke, and John). 3) Ask the Holy Spirit to help you understand God's heart in Scripture. Believe He will speak to you personally through the Bible. 4) Don't focus on what you don't understand, but concentrate on what God makes real to you.

BIBLICAL REASON #14

Galatians 3:1-5
Declarations keep us from reverting back to performance-based Christianity and the Law.

15 FREEDOM FROM ADDICTIVE BEHAVIORS

THE SCRIPTURE

"Therefore, if anyone is in Christ, he is a new creation; old things have passed away; behold, all things have become new" (2 Corinthians 5:17).

"Stand fast therefore in the liberty by which Christ has made us free, and do not be entangled again with a yoke of bondage" (Galatians 5:1).

THE DECLARATIONS

- I am not who my past experience says I am; I am who God says I am.

- I am not destined to struggle with the same addictions my parents or grandparents were bound by.

- At the cross I was made a new creation; therefore, I do not have to be influenced by any baggage of the past.

- I have been set free and released from all bondage through what Jesus has done for me.

- Every day I make the choice to walk in the freedom Jesus paid for me.

- I am free from condemnation, and during temptation I find God's strength working mightily in me.

- Today is the day of my breakthrough — I am free!

- Every generational curse was broken at the cross; therefore, I am victorious and free from addiction.

- I have powerful people in my life to help me walk in freedom.

- I am healed from every root that would cause me to walk in addictive behaviors.

THE BREAKING OFF OF AGREEMENT WITH THESE COMMON LIES

- My identity will always be connected with my addiction.

- I will never get free; I will always have to manage my addictive behavior.

THE WISDOM TO ADD TO DECLARATIONS

Silence the cravings — Speak to the craving as though it has ears and tell it to go. (Consider reading Steve's book *You're Crazy If You Don't Talk To Yourself* to more fully understand the concept of proclaiming your freedom through speaking life.)

Eliminate sources of temptation — Take the things that are tempting you out of your house, car, office, and routine. Decrease or stop your association with people who increase temptation in your life.

Draw on community — Seek out spiritual mentors and those who have had breakthrough in the same area of temptation. Connect with them as often as possible. Get them to pray for you and help keep you accountable. Also, feed on testimonies and stories of those who have overcome what you are battling.

BIBLICAL REASON #15

Judges 6:12
Declarations unlock destinies.

16 TIME MANAGEMENT

THE SCRIPTURE

"See then that you walk circumspectly, not as fools but as wise, redeeming the time, because the days are evil" (Ephesians 5:15-16).

"Make the most of every opportunity" (Colossians 4:5b).

THE DECLARATIONS

- I am increasingly able to accomplish more in less time.

- I have divine strategies and ideas for how to manage my time.

- I love taking time for important things, not just urgent things, in my life.

- I honor God with my time and fulfill all His purposes for my life.

- I walk with an awareness of how I'm investing my time.

- I have an exceptional ability to make the best use of my time.

- While making decisions on how to use my time, I think long-term and make decisions that bring me closer to life-long goals.

- I plan my days well and find scheduling enjoyable and easy.

- My time is a resource that I use strategically to accomplish all that I set out to do.

- I am a very reliable person, and I arrive early for appointments and meetings.

THE BREAKING OFF OF AGREEMENT WITH THESE COMMON LIES

- I'm not good at managing my time or accomplishing goals.

- I've tried to do this before and failed, so I know I can't do this.

THE WISDOM TO ADD TO DECLARATIONS

Take account of your time "spent" — Time is a resource, like money, which is why we say that we "spend" our time. Begin a time spending log. Break down each day into hours, and write how you "spend" each hour.

Evaluate what is important — Look at your time log and ask yourself if there are things you spend time on that are not a priority for you. Create plans to adjust your time accordingly.

Multi-task to accomplish more — Find ways to accomplish things by incorporating them into what you are already doing. Get creative. Are you evangelistic but don't have time to reach out? How about praying for one person each time you go shopping? Need to send birthday cards but are busy with the kids? How about having them help you?

BIBLICAL REASON #16

Job 22:28
Declarations establish what we desire to have in our lives.

17 RELEASING THE SUPERNATURAL

THE SCRIPTURE

"Now thanks be to God who always leads us in triumph in Christ, and through us diffuses the fragrance of His knowledge in every place" (2 Corinthians 2:14).

"Do you not know that you are the temple of God and that the Spirit of God dwells in you?" (1 Corinthians 3:16).

THE DECLARATIONS

- I am clothed with Christ, therefore I release His presence everywhere I go.

- I am so baptized in the Holy Spirit that I naturally spill over to those around me.

- My words impart grace to those who hear me.

- Angels get really excited when I show up because they get put to work.

- I have the mind of Christ and I use it.

- When I speak to non-believers, they are overcome with a sudden urge to get saved.

- It is impossible for me to pray and have nothing happen.

- I release the supernatural naturally and effortlessly.

- I think and speak prophetically.

- My touch releases the healing grace of Jesus.

THE BREAKING OFF OF AGREEMENT WITH THESE COMMON LIES

- Only super-anointed people release the supernatural, not common Christians.

- I have to spend many hours with God, read the Word constantly, and work really hard to release God's presence.

THE WISDOM TO ADD TO DECLARATIONS

Study every supernatural happening in the Book of Acts — Believe for these things in your own life and in the lives of those you influence.

Utilize biblical keys to release the supernatural — Those who value the power of extending forgiveness, declaring blessings, speaking truth, and praying with courage will truly bring heaven to earth.

When you pray, expect the supernatural to manifest — For instance, when you pray for someone, ask them what they felt or sensed. Also, remember that God is at work even if nothing appears to be happening.

BIBLICAL SUPPORT #17

Luke 4:18-21
Jesus began his supernatural ministry with declarations, so why wouldn't we?

18 TRAVEL AND MODES OF TRANSPORTATION

THE SCRIPTURE

"Blessed shall you be when you come in, and blessed shall you be when you go out" (Deuteronomy 28:6).

"A thousand may fall at your side, And ten thousand at your right hand; But it shall not come near you" (Psalm 91:7).

THE DECLARATIONS

- Those who ride in my vehicles encounter God's love and power.

- I have abundant finances to travel wherever God calls me to go.

- All of my vehicles glorify God and help advance the Kingdom.

- I make good decisions in buying cars, trucks, planes, and other means of travel. I receive astounding deals in these purchases.

- I am supernaturally protected from danger as I travel.

- The people who work on my vehicles are honest and skilled.

- Just as Philip was in Acts 8, I am transported in travel.

- Like Joshua, every place I go is impacted by my godly influence.

- Instead of experiencing jet lag, I have surprising energy when traveling into different time zones.

- My descendants are known for transportation inventions.

- I travel all around the world impacting people with the gospel.

THE BREAKING OFF OF AGREEMENT WITH THESE COMMON LIES

- Accidents and travel misfortunes are random events that cannot be decreased or eliminated in our family tree.

- There are no supernatural means of travel available to us.

THE WISDOM TO ADD TO DECLARATIONS

Believe for all supernatural biblical transportation experiences — Elijah ran faster than a chariot (1 Kings 18:44-46). Jesus and Peter walked on water (Matthew 14:22-33). Philip was transported (Acts 8:39-40). The Israelites went through a sea (Exodus 14:21-22). Jesus changed the weather for better travel (Mark 4:35-41).

Dedicate all your vehicles and all your travels to God — Regularly speak words of blessing over these.

Connect with gifted people — Before you buy vehicles, glean from the wisdom of others (people, websites, books, etc.).

BIBLICAL SUPPORT #18

Joshua 1:8
Declarations are instrumental for us to enter our "Promised Land."

19 STANDING FOR A CAUSE

THE SCRIPTURE

"But if serving the Lord seems undesirable to you, then choose for your-selves this day whom you will serve… But as for me and my household, we will serve the Lord" (Joshua 24:15).

"Our God whom we serve is able to deliver us from the burning fiery furnace, and He will deliver us from your hand, O king. But if not, let it be known to you, O king, that we do not serve your gods, nor will we worship the gold image which you have set up" (Daniel 3:17-18).

THE DECLARATIONS

- As for me and my house, we will serve the Lord.

- I have strong convictions in my life.

- I love truth and integrity more than money, fame, comfort, or success.

- I am a God-pleaser, not a people-pleaser.

- There are things I am willing to die for.

- I inspire others to stand up for truth.

- I sacrifice so others can be free.

- I am a person of principle.

- I have wisdom in how to communicate about the things I believe in.

- I am a very courageous person.

- People know me as a person who is passionate about a cause.

THE BREAKING OFF OF AGREEMENT WITH THESE COMMON LIES

- It is more important to be popular and financially successful than to be a person of principle.

- I have always been directed by others and find it difficult to stand up for what I believe in.

THE WISDOM TO ADD TO DECLARATIONS

Read about people who took a stand for a cause — There are many great examples (Winston Churchill, Abraham Lincoln, Martin Luther King, Charles Finney, Bill Johnson). Feed on the stories of those who were courageous and who made a difference. It will inspire you to do the same.

Live a life of sacrifice — Know that freedom is not free. It is the result of someone sacrificing comfort for the benefit of society and others. As we commit ourselves to making a difference, we will find the areas of life we are to be especially committed to.

Find ways to influence others about your cause — Educate others, but stay away from guilt and manipulation. Learn how to motivate through truth and vision. We can make a difference.

BIBLICAL SUPPORT #19

Matthew 8:8-13
The centurion (whom Jesus celebrated) understood the power of a declaration.

20   PARENTING

THE SCRIPTURE

"Train up a child in the way he should go; even when he is old he will not depart from it" (Proverbs 22:6).

"Behold, children are a heritage from the Lord; the fruit of the womb is a reward. Like arrows in the hand of a warrior, so are the children of one's youth. Happy is the man who has his quiver full of them; they shall not be ashamed" (Psalm 127:3-5).

THE DECLARATIONS

- I am a great parent.

- I am full of vision and hope for my children.

- It is easy to teach my kids the ways and principles of the Kingdom.

- Communication is simple and clear between my kids and me.

- I have an abundance of solutions and wisdom for every situation my family encounters.

- My children feel safe, free, and loved in our home.

- I am raising up powerful world-changers in my home.

- My offspring are known for strong families, wisdom, integrity, favor, miracles, health, courage, abundance, evangelism, honor, inventions, passion for the Bible, generosity, and love.

- My family tree is blessed and a blessing to the whole earth.

- I know how to discipline and empower my kids in ways that produce health and life.

- Future generations will be blessed and highly favored because of the way I am parenting my children today.

THE BREAKING OFF OF AGREEMENT WITH THESE COMMON LIES

- My kids and I are disconnected, and it is impossible to reconnect.

- I do not have what it takes to raise godly children who change the world.

THE WISDOM TO ADD TO DECLARATIONS

Prioritize having a strong heart connection with your child — Take advantage of these special times with your son or daughter: bedtime, meal times, driving in the car, doing projects together, walks after they have had a challenging day, etc.

Become a learner — It is never too late to read a book or listen to a teaching on parenting to improve your practical and philosophical skills. It is the wise parent who annually does something specific to grow in his or her parenting skills.

Partner with others in the nurturing of your children — Find a good children's ministry or youth group for your child. Invest in their future by having them attend a powerful camp each year. Enlist other parents and older children to be a positive influence on your family.

BIBLICAL SUPPORT #20

Matthew 12:36
Declarations are the opposite of speaking idle words.

21 COMMUNICATION AND CONFLICT RESOLUTION

THE SCRIPTURE

"A word fitly spoken is like apples of gold in settings of silver. Like an earring of gold and an ornament of fine gold is a wise man's rebuke to an obedient ear" (Proverbs 25:11-12).

"Let no corrupt word proceed from your mouth except what is good for necessary edification that it may impart grace to the hearers" (Ephesians 4:29).

THE DECLARATIONS

- I am a great communicator.

- I express my thoughts and feelings easily.

- I always know what to say, and my tone and body language line up with what I am communicating.

- I have supernatural wisdom in the area of conflict resolution. I know when I should and should not address a matter.

- I always seek to understand other peoples' hearts before addressing issues with them.

- My relationships are strong because I have cultivated a freedom from the fear of confrontation in my life.

- I joyfully embrace opportunities to resolve conflict with others.

- My value for healthy communication and conflict resolution has set a positive example to my friends, family, and colleagues of what good relationships look like.

- I value relationship above the pain or inconvenience of confrontation.

- When others seek to resolve conflict with me, I am open, receptive and willing to make necessary changes in my life.

THE BREAKING OFF OF AGREEMENT WITH THESE COMMON LIES

- I always say the wrong thing and people have a tendency to misunderstand me.

- It is more spiritual and mature to just let issues go rather than to bring them up with others.

THE WISDOM TO ADD TO DECLARATIONS

Prioritize developing your communication skills — Participate in regular training to improve your communication and conflict resolution abilities. Read books on the subject. Get feedback from someone you trust on how you are doing.

Learn to ask great questions of others — Many conflicts result from misunderstandings. Before you assume you know what is happening, ask questions to help in the process. Often the seeming current problem is not the real issue, and there is something deeper and more important to be discovered through a person who is mature enough to try to understand.

Learn to thrive when experiencing unresolved relationship issues – Sometimes, no matter what we do, there are people in our lives who don't like us, disagree with us or are causing conflict in our world. Part of our maturing as a person and a Christian is to not allow this to neutralize our forward movement in life.

BIBLICAL SUPPORT #21

I Peter 3:10
He who would love life and see good days will make declarations.

22 HEALTH AND WELL BEING

THE SCRIPTURE

"But they who wait for the Lord shall renew their strength; they shall mount up with wings like eagles; they shall run and not be weary; they shall walk and not faint" (Isaiah 40:31).

A joyful heart is good medicine." (Proverbs 17:22).

THE DECLARATIONS

- I walk in ever-increasing health.

- It is easy for me to prioritize exercise into my daily schedule.

- I drink plenty of water every day.

- I am highly motivated and full of energy to accomplish everything I need to do today.

- I laugh easily and often and find joy in every day life knowing that it brings health and life (see Proverbs 17:22).

- My health and well-being matters to God even more than it matters to me.

- My healthiest days are ahead of me.

- My family is blessed with divine health and well-being.

- I am experiencing health in my mind, emotions, and body.

- I make great choices about food, and I enjoy eating healthy every day.

THE BREAKING OFF OF AGREEMENT WITH THESE COMMON LIES

- My health and well-being are not spiritual enough for me to give time and energy toward.

- Seeing change and improvement in my health has been difficult in the past, so wanting to try again is pointless.

THE WISDOM TO ADD TO DECLARATIONS

Take time to dream with God — Make goals for your health and well-being. Stir your faith with what is possible.

Begin with small steps — You could choose to drink water instead of sugary beverages, take 15 minutes to walk outside, or do some strength-building exercises. Celebrate your progress, just not perfection!

Educate yourself regularly about health and well-being — Make it your goal to continually learn and be inspired about these subjects by attending seminars, reading, visiting websites and building relationships with those who value health in every area of life.

BIBLICAL SUPPORT #22

Joel 3:10
Let the weak say, "I am strong."

23 WISDOM AND INTELLIGENCE

THE SCRIPTURE

"Then the king interviewed them... And in all matters of wisdom and understanding . . . he found them ten times better than all the magicians and astrologers who were in all his realm" (Daniel 1:19-20).

"For God has . . . given us . . . a sound mind" (2 Timothy 1:7).

"We have the mind of Christ" (1 Corinthians 2:16).

THE DECLARATIONS

- God has given me extraordinary wisdom, understanding, and knowledge.

- I have divine strategies and ideas for every area of life.

- I love to learn, and it comes easily to me.

- I think clearly, quickly, and with God's heart in every matter.

- I excel in educational environments.

- Brilliant, societal-transforming thinkers are in my lineage.

- My descendants include authors, scientists, inventors, teachers, innovators, and great leaders.

- I think as Jesus thinks.

- My mind is being renewed to think in powerful ways.

- I walk in revelation knowledge of all matters in life.

THE BREAKING OFF OF AGREEMENT WITH THESE COMMON LIES

- The most spiritual people are those who are smarter and wiser than me.

- It is impossible for me to walk in supernatural wisdom and understanding.

THE WISDOM TO ADD TO DECLARATIONS

Study the life and writings of Solomon — Even though he ended poorly, Solomon's supernatural insight and resulting abundance represents what we can become today.

Ask and believe God for extraordinary wisdom and understanding — James 1:5-8 gives a guarantee that if we ask in faith for wisdom, we will receive an abundant amount.

Know the fear of the Lord is the beginning point for true knowledge and wisdom (see Proverbs 1:7; 9:10) — Humility and acknowledging God releases true understanding.

BIBLICAL SUPPORT #23

Romans 4:17
Declarations help us call those things that are not as though they are.

24 MEETINGS I WILL LEAD

THE SCRIPTURE

"I can do all things through Christ who strengthens me" (Philippians 4:13).

"And whatever he does shall prosper" (Psalm 1:3).

THE DECLARATIONS

- I lead a powerful life and lead powerful meetings.

- People eagerly desire to be a part of meetings I lead.

- I thoroughly enjoy preparing for meetings, and I am ecstatically confident in my ability to lead them.

- People in my family, church, and organization know they will encounter God's love, goodness, and power in the meetings I lead.

- The meetings I hold are a key to the success of my organization.

- I successfully lead diverse kinds of people in meetings.

- When I leave meetings, I feel an overwhelming sense of satisfaction for all that was accomplished.

- I have a unique ability to get things done while having healthy relationships with the other leaders in my meetings.

- I carefully consider the input from all those on my team.

- I have great wisdom in dealing with problems and unexpected happenings in the meetings I lead.

THE BREAKING OFF OF AGREEMENT WITH THESE COMMON LIES

- I am not good at leading meetings and dread planning them.

- I am the only one on my team with wisdom and good ideas.

THE WISDOM TO ADD TO DECLARATIONS

Create an agenda — This forces preparation and aids in time management, making it possible to touch on vital items before the time is up.

Take action — Take notes and notate everything needing to be done after the meeting. Assign a team member to each item and send them reminders. At your next meeting, ask for a status report on all the action items.

Plan to give God room to move — Be conscious of the Lord and ask God for creative ways to bring Him into the meeting. One of the keys to doing this is to avoid cramming too many things into one meeting.

BIBLICAL SUPPORT #24

Romans 6:11
Declarations help us to stay grounded in truth.

25   HEALING

THE SCRIPTURE

"Forget not all His benefits… Who heals all your diseases" (Psalm 103:2-3).

"But He was pierced for our transgressions, He was crushed for our iniquities; the punishment that brought us peace was on Him, and by His wounds we are healed" (Isaiah 53:5).

THE DECLARATIONS

- Jesus is the same yesterday, today, and forever. He still likes to heal.

- There are no walls between the healing grace of Jesus and me.

- My body is under supernatural protection.

- By His stripes I have already been healed.

- I am a magnet for healing, and people around me constantly get healed.

- I am worthy to walk in divine health through the blood of Jesus.

- It is extremely easy for people in my region of the world to get healed.

- I am immune to sickness and disease because I am a new creation with new DNA.

- My family and I are free from generational illnesses through a divine swap of our inheritance for Jesus' inheritance.

- I am living in ever increasing health. My eyes, bones, hearing, central nervous system, organs, and muscles get stronger and stronger the longer I live.

THE BREAKING OFF OF AGREEMENT WITH THESE COMMON LIES

- God gives sickness and disease to teach us lessons.

- God cares about our spirits and souls but not our bodies because they are only temporary.

THE WISDOM TO ADD TO DECLARATIONS

Keep testimonies of healing in front of you and talk about them regularly — The word "testimony" means to do again. When you declare a testimony, you release the same power of God that was released in the original healing to be released in yourself.

Be relentless in praying for those needing healing — Releasing healing to others is similar to developing muscle. The more you exercise imparting healing, the greater breakthrough you will see. Be encouraged, some who have a great healing ministry today did not always see the same results when they first began.

Study diligently and believe in the finished works of the cross — Healing truly is one of the benefits of our salvation. Our faith for healing is rooted in God's goodness as demonstrated in Scripture.

BIBLICAL SUPPORT #25

Hebrews 10:23
We are called to be incessant hope speakers, and declarations help make this a reality in our lives.

26 REST AND SLEEPING

THE SCRIPTURE

"I will both lie down in peace, and sleep" (Psalm 4:8).

"When you lie down, you will not be afraid. Yes, you will lie down and your sleep will be sweet" (Proverbs 3:24).

THE DECLARATIONS

- I am an amazing sleeper.

- As soon as my head hits the pillow, I fall asleep.

- I sleep deeply and soundly right through the night.

- I have encounters with God as I sleep.

- Each morning, I wake up feeling refreshed, full of energy, and overflowing with excitement for the day.

- Even in the midst of the most difficult circumstances, I have an ability to enter into His rest.

- I have powerful life-changing dreams when I sleep.

- I have an anointing to help others be blessed in their sleep.

- I am protected in my sleep from bad dreams.

- I consistently work from a place of resting in Him.

THE BREAKING OFF OF AGREEMENT WITH THESE COMMON LIES

- I will only be able to rest once I get everything done.

- Some people are just bad sleepers.

THE WISDOM TO ADD TO DECLARATIONS

Believe, through Jesus' work on the cross, we have entered into a New Covenant of rest — The Promised Land in the Old Covenant was also known as a land of God's rest (see Hebrews 3:11). Jesus has delivered us into the New Covenant Promised Land of God's rest. Psalm 110:1 says "Sit at my right hand, till I make your enemies your footstool." God does not say we have to wait until every problem is taken care of before we rest – He says rest first, and He will make our enemies our footstool.

Calm your mind before going to bed — Don't engage in any mentally stimulating activities, but meditate on Scripture. It will center you on God and help still your mind.

Resist the temptation to speak about being tired — This is not to deny how we are feeling, but when we are tired, it can be easy to continually speak this out and contribute to a perpetual state of tiredness. Let us be intentional about our words.

BIBLICAL SUPPORT #26

Mark 11:24 and I John 5:14-15
Declarations are a way for us to pray believing prayers.

27 FAMILY RELATIONSHIPS

THE SCRIPTURE

"Behold, I am the Lord, the God of all flesh. Is anything too difficult for Me?" (Jeremiah 32:27).

"Now to Him who is able to do far more abundantly than all we ask or think." (Ephesians 3:20).

THE DECLARATIONS

- I have great hope for every member of my family.

- God is completely committed to all of my family relationships, and He is at work doing more than I see.

- Each person in my family has a high calling to bring the Kingdom of God to the world around them.

- My family walks in ever increasing revelation of the goodness and love of God toward them.

- My family connections are going deeper and becoming more significant every day.

- The Father is using my family relationships in significant ways to impact the world.

- The best seasons of my family life are ahead.

- It is easy for me to have significant conversations and to share my heart with every person in my family.

- The prayers I pray for my family members are powerful, effective, and they are changing my family's destiny.

- All my family members are great decision makers whose choices bring health and prosperity to them and their descendants.

THE BREAKING OFF OF AGREEMENT WITH THESE COMMON LIES

- My family relationships will never improve.

- God does not care about changing my family as much as He cares about changing the world.

THE WISDOM TO ADD TO DECLARATIONS

Take time to connect with every member of your family — Don't underestimate the power of consistent connection through email, letters, or short phone calls.

Be your family's greatest encourager — Nothing will bring more life to your family than encouragement. See them with eyes of hope, and share with them what you see.

Prioritize teachings that will help you in family relationships — We can never get enough wisdom and encouragement to help us be successful in relating to our families. Unfortunately, many wait until a crisis occurs to get serious about investing intentionally in their most important relationships.

BIBLICAL SUPPORT #27

Genesis 1:2-3
Declarations give the Holy Spirit something to work with to accomplish God's will.

28 IMPARTATION

THE SCRIPTURE

"Do not neglect the gift that is in you, which was given to you by prophecy with the laying on of the hands of the eldership" (1 Timothy 4:14).

"For I long to see you, that I may impart to you some spiritual gift, so that you may be established" (Romans 1:11).

"Now Joshua the son of Nun was full of the spirit of wisdom, for Moses had laid his hands on him…" (Deuteronomy 34:9).

THE DECLARATIONS

- I become more established in my life by receiving impartation from others.

- Others seek me out to give me what I did not earn. I am an impartation magnet.

- When I declare life or lay hands on people, they are launched into higher dimensions of life and ministry.

- I carry more than I am aware of due to the impartations I have received.

- I have an expectation to do more than I have before because of what I have received from others.

- God provides shortcuts for those who believe and receive.

- I am able to prophesy, heal the sick, raise the dead, cleanse leapers, walk in increased wisdom, boldness, and creativity through the act of the cross and impartation.

- As I honor the gifts of others, I am able to receive the same gifts and build on them.

- I have the ability to give away what God has given me to those who earnestly desire spiritual gifts.

THE BREAKING OFF OF AGREEMENT WITH THESE COMMON LIES

- If God wants me to have a gift, He will give it to me directly. He will not use another person in order to do so.

- Only Christian superstars can impart to others, not people like me.

THE WISDOM TO ADD TO DECLARATIONS

Intentionally pursue impartations — Develop relationships with people who are strong influencers or who are walking powerfully in the gifts of the Spirit. Go to healing/miracle/prophetic meetings or schools in pursuit of impartations.

List the impartations you have received — Frequently review this list as a reminder of what you have received and carry in your life.

Create a plan to regularly impart to others — Ask God to show you what you have that others need. Then get a strategy to consistently impart this to others in a natural way.

BIBLICAL SUPPORT #28

I Samuel 17:27, 46-47
Giant killers make declarations.

29 WEALTHY LIVING

THE SCRIPTURE

"And you shall remember the Lord your God, for it is He who gives you power to get wealth, that He may establish His covenant which He swore to your fathers, as it is this day" (Deuteronomy 8:18).

"The rich man's wealth is his strong city. The destruction of the poor is their poverty" (Proverbs 10:15).

THE DECLARATIONS

- In every area of my life, I live in abundance.

- I am blessed to be a blessing.

- I have more then enough to sow into the Kingdom of God.

- I make great financial decisions.

- The distribution of my wealth becomes the answer to the prayers of those in need.

- The favor of God weighs so heavily on my life that I am perpetually moving in the right direction to be a blessing to others.

- I have divine wisdom and insight when making decisions about my finances.

- The wealth that I accrue in my life will be a blessing to my children's children's children.

- God desires for me to prosper financially.

- Whenever I have financial gain, I re-invest well and give generously.

THE BREAKING OFF OF AGREEMENT WITH THESE COMMON LIES

- God has predestined a few people to be wealthy, and I am not one of them.
- I cannot be trusted with wealth, so God won't give it to me.

THE WISDOM TO ADD TO DECLARATIONS

Develop an abundance theology — It is impossible to do what God has called us to do without abundance. If we are going to influence the nations with the gospel (see Matthew 28:18-20), we need an abundance of health, energy, finances, favor, wisdom, power, love, and protection so we can accomplish it.

Learn how money works — In the Parable of the Talents found in Matthew 25:13-15, the master gives talents (money) to three people. There is an expectation that each develop the wisdom to increase what they are given. We too can learn how to do this. It is the wise person who partakes of teaching by such people as Dave Ramsey, Steve DeSilva, or others who have great knowledge in how financial breakthrough happens.

Overcome the debt mentality, and then invest — Those with the debt mentality sacrifice the future for the desires of today. Financial debt is usually a symptom of a deeper issue that impulsively prioritizes urgent, but not important, choices in life. Those who have an investment mindset focus more on the important but not urgent matters. We can all learn to choose these higher priorities.

BIBLICAL SUPPORT #29

2 Corinthians 10:4-5
Declarations are a key to demolishing strongholds.

30 LEAVING A LEGACY & AN ENDURING INHERITANCE

THE SCRIPTURE

"A good man leaves an inheritance to his children's children"
(Proverbs 13:22).

"So Moses swore on that day, saying, 'Surely the land where your foot has trodden shall be your inheritance and your children's forever, because you have wholly followed the Lord my God'" (Joshua 14:9).

THE DECLARATIONS

- I am leaving a bountiful inheritance to my descendants, and to the people, ministries, workplaces, cities, and nations that I am a part of.

- My descendants adore Jesus and release His love and salvation throughout the earth.

- My life causes a dramatic, positive change in my family tree and in the ministries, cities, and nations that I am a part of.

- The lives of my family and descendants are protected from disaster, disease, divorce, adultery, abuse, poverty, false accusation, foolish decisions, and all accidents.

- Generational blessings from the past are increasingly manifesting in each new generation of my family.

- My family produces great leaders in every sphere of society.

- My offspring are known for integrity, wisdom, favor, generosity, love, courage, abundance, honor, and health.

- My descendants flow in the power of evangelism and the working of miracles. They have a love for the Bible, strong families, and minds to create life-changing inventions.

- My family tree is blessed and is a blessing to the whole earth.

THE BREAKING OFF OF AGREEMENT WITH THESE COMMON LIES

- Things will never change in my family.

- What happens in my lifetime is the most important thing.

THE WISDOM TO ADD TO DECLARATIONS

Study diligently and believe in the finished works of the cross — Abraham was "strengthened in faith" to become "fully convinced" of what was promised. (See Romans 4:20-21.) As a result, he left an incredible inheritance. As we believe our promises, we will too.

Think generationally — Scripture reveals that God develops His long term plans through multiple generations. Long-term thinkers are the most emotionally healthy because they see the bigger picture of what is happening.

Start releasing your inheritance now — Share eternal values with those you love and develop a plan to create wealth. Also, believe in the power of your prayers to affect future generations.

BIBLICAL SUPPORT #30

Romans 12:2
The making of declarations is one of the most practical ways to renew our minds.

WRITING YOU OWN DECLARATIONS

One of the main purposes of this book is to help you create your own declarations for important areas of your life. The next few pages are designed to help you get started in this.

Lies I Am Tempted To Believe

Romans 15:13 says, "Now may the God of hope fill you with all joy and peace in believing, that you may abound in hope by the power fo the Holy Spirit." When we believe truth, our hope will rise. Therefore, our hope level in an area of life determines whether we are believing lies or truth. If we have glistening hope, we are believing truth. If we do not have hope in an area, we are probably believing lies.

Are there some areas of your life that are not glistening with hope?.

....

....

....

....

....

....

....

....

....

Relevant Bible Verses

What does Scripture say about this particular area of your life? Try looking up topics similar to your area of emphasis in a concordance or online. Write one to three verses here.

My Declarations

Now begin making declarations based on what God has said, or is saying. If you're having a difficult time, just skim through some of the declarations we have made already to help give you some ideas of how to make your own declarations. Write as many here as you like, but aim for at least five.

OFFERING READINGS AND OTHER DECLARATIONS

The following declarations are used during the offering times at Bethel Church, in Redding, California, and numerous other churches across the globe. We encourage you to begin making declarations over your own offerings.

You may find these offering readings online at:

http://www.ibethel.org/offering-readings

OFFERING OF THANKS #1

As we receive today's offering we are believing the Lord for:
Jobs and better jobs; Raises and bonuses;
Benefits, Sales and Commissions ; Favorable settlements;
Estates and inheritances ; Interests and income;
Rebates and returns; Checks in the mail;
Gifts and surprises; Finding money; Debts paid off;
Expenses decrease; Blessing and increase.

Thank You, Lord, for meeting all of my financial needs
that I may have more than enough
to give into the Kingdom of God
and promote the Gospel of Jesus Christ.
Hallelujah!

OFFERING OF THANKS #2

As we receive today's offering, we are believing You for:
Heaven opened, Earth Invaded, Storehouses unlocked,
and Miracles created;
Dreams and Visions, Angelic Visitations,
Declarations, Impartations, and Divine Manifestations;
Anointings, Gifting, and Calls, Positions, and Promotions;
Provisions and Resources to go to the nations;
Souls and more souls from every generation,
Saved and set free, Carrying Kingdom revelation!

Thank You, Father, that as I join my value system to Yours,
You will shower FAVOR, BLESSINGS and INCREASE
upon me so I have more than enough
to co-labor with Heaven and see
JESUS get His FULL REWARD.
Hallelujah!

OFFERING OF THANKS #3

As we pray for new wells of revival,
we pray for new economic wells in Redding to be created.
So Lord we ask you for:
Favor for our city with CEO's, Government leaders & Kings.
Manufacturing firms that produce goods for the nations
and provide new jobs for our people.
Technology to establish new markets, energy sources,
and efficient solutions to grow as a population.
Laws & Courts that measure with the justice and the freedom
of our land's Constitution.
Civil servants that encourage entrepreneurs.
Media known for wisdom & truth.
Natural resources released, harvested, sold & reproduced.
Education, books, and Universities that develop
mind-molders who influence the influential.
Capital to build small businesses that provide services,
arts and culture, attracting both young and old.
Medical community known for integrity and excellence.
Repentance from poverty, small thinking, and envy.
Courage to recognize opportunities and make wealth.
Abundance to bless the world
and the prudence to save and invest.
Revelation to pass on wealth to our children's children…

So we declare that when the righteous prosper, the city rejoices!

OFFERING OF THANKS #4
(Children's Ministry)

I am powerful, and what I believe changes the world!
So today I declare:
God is in a good mood.
He loves me all the time.
Nothing can separate me from His love.
Jesus' blood paid for everything.
I will tell nations of what He has done.
I am important.
How He made me is amazing.
I was designed for worship.
My mouth establishes praise to silence the enemy.
Everywhere I go becomes a perfect health zone.
And with God,
Nothing is impossible!

DECLARATION OVER THE NATIONS

Thank you Lord that You are the hope of the nations and You will build Your church around the world.

We call to the nations in the North, the South, the East and the West and we declare:

JESUS IS LORD! No weapon formed against them will stand!

We release angelic activity with power, signs and wonders. We cast down injustices, evil mindsets, corruption, poverty, disease and hopelessness. We speak grace, peace, breakthrough and healing over the land. We call for justice and reconciliation.

We ask that government leaders will have:

– Holy Spirit inspired, supernatural encounters and dreams.
– Wisdom, discernment, knowledge to make righteous governmental decisions.

We ask that church leaders and believers will have:

– Extreme hunger for God, new revelations, thoughts and ideas.
– Righteous decisions.
– Courage, wisdom, discernment, and knowledge of how to lead Your people.
– Unity among the young and old.
– Demonic assignments broken and lives mended.
– Divine protection and favor.
– Abundance and provision.
– New leaders being raised up to carry revival fire.
– Extreme hunger for God, new revelations, thoughts and ideas.

Encourage and bless the nations and Your people with peace and display Your extravagant favor and love to them.

We call for revival fire to come!

DECLARATION OVER MISSIONARIES

Thank you Lord for the missionaries and their families.

We ask that You would:

- Encourage them by Your Word and promises.
- Give them understanding, wisdom, insight and FRESH revelation.
- Help them to be strong in supernatural strength and ability.
- May signs and wonders follow them wherever they go.
- We pray for open doors of ministry, necessary visa's, permits and extraordinary language aptitude.
- Give divine favor and connections. Open doors that no man can shut and make the impossible, possible.
- Comfort them in times of loneliness.
- Give them friends and relationships with like hearted people.
- Lift them above every obstacle that appears before them.
- Give them dreams in the night seasons from Your heart.

We cut off every assignment from the enemy and we speak breakthrough in every area that is causing discouragement, fear or doubt.

We ask for Your peace and joy to invade their circumstances.

We speak divine protection and good health over them.

We ask for provision spiritually, emotionally, physically and financially.

We speak victory over them and bless, bless, bless them Lord Jesus!

ADDITIONAL RESOURCES

Victorious Mindsets

What we believe is ultimately more important than what we do. The course of our lives is set by our deepest core beliefs. Our mindsets are either a stronghold for God's purposes or a playhouse for the enemy. In this book, fifty biblical attitudes are revealed that are foundational for those who desire to walk in freedom and power.

Cracks in the Foundation

Going to a higher level in establishing key beliefs will affect ones intimacy with God and fruitfulness for the days ahead. This book challenges many basic assumptions of familiar Bible verses and common Christian phrases that block numerous benefits of our salvation. The truths shared in this book will help fill and repair "cracks" in our thinking which rob us of our God-given potential.

You're Crazy If You Don't Talk to Yourself

Jesus did not just think His way out of the wilderness and neither can we. He spoke truth to invisible beings and mindsets that sought to restrict and defeat Him. This book reveals that life and death are truly in the power of the tongue, and emphasize the necessity of speaking truth to our souls. Our words really do set the course of our lives and the lives of others. (Proverbs 18:21; James 3:2-5)

Let's Just Laugh at That

Our hope level is an indicator of whether we are believing truth or lies. Truth creates hope and freedom, but believing lies brings hopelessness and restriction. We can have great theology but still be powerless because of deception about the key issues of life.

Many of these self-defeating mindsets exist in our subconscious and have never been identified. This book exposes numerous falsehoods and reveals truth that makes us free. Get ready for a joy-infused adventure into hope-filled living.

Divine Strategies for Increase

The laws of the spirit are more real than the natural laws. God's laws are primarily principles to release blessing, not rules to be obeyed to gain right standing with God. The Psalmist talks of one whose greatest delight is in the law of the Lord. This delight allows one to discover new aspects of the nature of God (hidden in each law) to behold and worship. The end result of this delighting is a transformed life that prospers in every endeavor. His experience can be our experience, and this book unlocks the blessings hidden in the spiritual realm.

Possessing Joy

In His presence is fullness of joy (Psalm 16:11). Joy is to increase as we go deeper in our relationship with God. Religious tradition has devalued the role that gladness and laughter have for personal victory and Kingdom advancement. His presence may not always produce joy; but if we never or rarely have fullness of joy, we must reevaluate our concept of God. This book takes one on a journey toward the headwaters of the full joy that Jesus often spoke of. Get ready for joy to increase and strength and longevity to ignite.

Igniting Faith in 40 Days

There must be special seasons in our lives when we break out of routine and do something that will ignite our faith about God and our identity in Christ. This book will lead you through the life-changing experience of a 40-day negativity fast. This fast teaches the power of declaring truth and other transforming daily customs that will strengthen your foundation of faith and radically increase your personal hope.

Living From The Unseen

This book will help you identify beliefs that block the reception of God's blessings and hinder our ability to live out our destiny. This book reveals that 1) Believing differently, not trying harder, is the key to change; 2) You cannot do what you don't believe you are.; 3) You can only receive what you think you are worth; 4) Rather than learning how to die — it is time to learn how to live..

Audio message series are available through the Igniting Hope store at:

www.IgnitingHope.com